LES
FLEURS DU MAL
AND OTHER STUDIES

AMS PRESS
NEW YORK

LES
FLEURS DU MAL

AND OTHER STUDIES

BY

ALGERNON CHARLES SWINBURNE

Edited with an Introduction by
EDMUND GOSSE, C.B.

LONDON:
PRINTED FOR PRIVATE CIRCULATION
1913

Library of Congress Cataloging in Publication Data

Swinburne, Algernon Charles, 1837–1909.
  Les fleurs du mal and other studies.

  Reprint. Originally printed: London, 1913.
  Contents: Les fleurs du mal — The golden age — La sieste de Jeanne — [etc.]
  1. French poetry—19th century—History and criticism—Addresses, essays, lectures. 2. English literature—19th century—History and criticism—Addresses, essays, lectures. I. Gosse, Edmund, 1849–1928. II. Title.
PQ438.S9 1985   840'.9'008   77-11487
ISBN 0-404-16347 5

AMS PRESS, INC.
56 East 13th Street, New York, N.Y. 10003

Reprinted courtesy of Indiana University, Bloomington, Indiana, from their copy, edition of 1913, London. Trim size has been slightly altered. Original trim: 12 x 18 cm.

MANUFACTURED IN THE UNITED STATES
OF AMERICA

LES FLEURS DU MAL

AND OTHER STUDIES

INTRODUCTION

THE seven studies which are here for the first time recovered from the periodicals to which they were originally contributed, are of diverse importance and extend over no fewer than thirty-four years. They display the prose style and the critical temper of Swinburne at various moments in youth and in old age, and they are alike only in the pleasant feature of enthusiasm which all display. He was a man who, if he praised, did not stint his praise. He was never content to sprinkle his eulogy grain by grain, but he poured out on the altar of the idol the whole fragrant bag of frankincense. There never has lived a more generous admirer of what he believed to be genius in others, and whatever may prove to be the ultimate authority of his judgments, they must always be valuable as throwing light on his own ardent character.

Of these seven studies by far the most weighty is the first, which introduced to English readers, so long ago as 1862, the name of Charles Baudelaire. This was the earliest excursion into serious prose criticism which Swinburne made, and it marks his earliest discovery. It required great intellectual courage in 1862 to champion in an English periodical the merits of any new volume of French verse, not to speak of such a volume as the *Fleurs du Mal*. England had not yet emerged from its long attack of Podsnappery, and there was hardly a critic of authority who ventured to advance the claims of French poetry. Victor Hugo's fame was that of a novelist, Lamartine's that of a politician, to the average Englishman. Vigny was absolutely unknown, and the English notion of French lyric was bounded by the fame of Beranger and Musset, whom Swinburne hated. The opening paragraphs of the essay on *Les Fleurs du Mal* must be read with a recollection of what a blank the mind of English readers of 1862 was on the general subject of recent French literature.

It is not certain by what means Swinburne met with the poems of Baudelaire. The Parisian history of the book must be briefly recounted, as it forms a curious episode in literary history. *Les Fleurs du Mal*, Baudelaire's first and most important publication, the work on which his fame mainly rests, was issued early in June, 1857. It immediately attracted violent praise and still more violent censure. In July it was prosecuted for offences against morality and decency, and a controversy arose in the newspapers, when Baudelaire's side was taken by the official journal, *Le Moniteur*. He was supported, publicly and privately, by the leading men of letters of the age, by Victor Hugo, Alfred de Vigny, Flaubert, Gautier, Leconte de Lisle, Sainte-Beuve. At the trial, he was ably defended by Maître Chaix d'Est-Ange, but in vain. In August, 1857, the court ordered poet and publisher to pay fines, and forbade the further issue of the book unless six specified poems were removed. Poulet-Malassis, the publisher, tried to go on issuing copies of the volume with the six incriminated pieces cut out! But purchasers were naturally indignant, and Baudelaire wrote to him (Oct. 9, 1857), "Si vous pouviez comprendre quel tort vous vous êtes fait avec votre ridicule opération chirurgicale!" The remainder of the mutilated edition was therefore destroyed, and *Les Fleurs du Mal* of 1857 became an exceedingly rare book.

It appears that Swinburne had not seen a copy of it when he wrote his study. This seems certain from the fact that he mentions none of the suppressed pieces, "Les Épaves," as they were afterwards called. Two of them, *Les Femmes Damnées* and *Lesbos*, he would unquestionably have mentioned; and these, I think, he must have become acquainted with, perhaps in a Brussels piracy, before he published *Poems and*

Ballads in 1866. Meanwhile, in Paris itself, there was a great deal of unsatisfied curiosity about Baudelaire. In 1859 Baudelaire began to speak of a second edition of *Les Fleurs du Mal*, but the publisher was extremely timid: at length, towards the end of January, 1861, he picked up courage enough to issue a small second edition, of course with "Les Épaves" omitted. This, there can be no doubt, is the form in which Swinburne first read Baudelaire, and in which he reviewed him for startled subscribers to the *Spectator*.

How he obtained possession of the book is at present doubtful. Swinburne told me that he wrote the review "in a Turkish bath," and I thought he said "in Paris." But was he in Paris until March, 1863? It is more probable that Monckton Milnes, who had a broad mind and a Parisian correspondence, possessed himself of a copy of the book and recommended, or lent it, to Swinburne. In a letter from Baudelaire to Whistler (not dated, but probably written in October, 1863), the former speaks of Swinburne in a way which suggests that, by that time at least, the French poet had been addressed by his English admirer through the intermediary of Whistler. This refers to the fact that in September, 1862, Swinburne had written to Baudelaire, whether through Whistler or through the painter, Fantin-

Latour, expressing his admiration and enclosing the unsigned review which we reprint. Of this letter and missive Baudelaire for a whole year, from indolence, made no acknowledgment whatever. He was conscious of his fault and bewailed to Whistler, "tout mon repentir de mon oubli et de mon apparente ingratitude."

But it has hitherto not been known that he did at length throw off his apathy and write to his English admirer. The occasion was a visit Félix Nadar was about to pay to London, where he had no acquaintances, and where Baudelaire, it seems, had none but Whistler and Swinburne. To the latter he wrote as follows:

A Monsieur Algernon Charles Swinburne.
16 Cheyne Walk, Chelsea, London.
10 *Octobre* 1863.

Monsieur,

Un de mes plus vieux amis va à Londres, M. Nadar, que vous aurez sans doute quelque plaisir à connaître. Je vous prie de vouloir bien faire pour lui tout ce que vous auriez fait sans doute pour moi, si j'étais allé m'adresser au public de votre patrie. Indications, conseils, réclames, il a besoin de beaucoup de choses.

Je sais infiniment de gré à Nadar de m'avoir demandé des lettres pour mes très rares accointances de Londres, car il m'a ainsi forcé de m'acquitter vis-à-vis de vous d'une grosse dette depuis longtemps non payée . . . je veux parler du merveilleux article (sur les *Fleurs du Mal*) que vous avez produit en Septembre 1862 dans le *Spectator*.

Un jour, M. Richard Wagner m'a sauté au cou pour me remercier d'une brochure que j'avais faite sur *Tannhäuser*, et m'a dit : " Je n'aurais jamais cru qu'un littérateur français pût comprendre si facilement tant de choses." N'étant pas exclusivement patriote, j'ai pris de son compliment tout ce qu'il avait de gracieux.

Permettez-moi, à mon tour, de vous dire : " Je n'aurais jamais cru qu'un littérateur anglais pût si bien pénétrer la beauté française, les intentions françaises et la prosodie française." Mais après la lecture des vers imprimés dans le même numero (" August ") et pénétré d'un sentiment à la fois si réel et si subtil, je n'ai pas été étonné du tout : il n'y a que les poètes pour bien comprendre les poètes.

Permettez-moi, cependant, de vous dire que vous avez poussé un peu loin ma défense. Je ne suis pas si *moraliste* que vous feignez obligeamment de le croire. Je crois simplement, comme vous sans doute, que tout poème, tout objet d'art *bien fait* suggère naturellement et forcément une *morale*. C'est l'affaire du lecteur. J'ai même une haine très décidée contre toute *intention* morale exclusive dans un poème.

Ayez la bonté de m'envoyer ce que vous publiez : j'y prendrai un grand plaisir. J'ai plusieurs livres à publier, je vous les expédierai successivement.

Veuillez agréer, Monsieur, l'expression très vive de ma gratitude et de ma sympathie.

CHARLES BAUDELAIRE.

A Paris, 22 rue d' Amsterdam.
A Honfleur, rue de Neubourg.

Je suis à Paris jusqu'à la fin de ce mois et je passerai tout décembre à Bruxelles.

This letter, so important as a statement of Baudelaire's own position, unfortunately never reached Swinburne, and was found last year, unopened, in a drawer. Baudelaire presently forwarded his brochure on Wagner, and this seems to have been the only

INTRODUCTION

communication Swinburne ever received from him. Baudelaire, retiring to Brussels, sank into a pitiable state of softening of the brain. He lingered wretchedly for many months. In April, 1867, Fantin-Latour mentioned to Swinburne the rumour that Baudelaire was dead, and he immediately composed his noble elegy, *Ave atque Vale*. Baudelaire survived, however, until August 31st, never having seen *Poems and Ballads*, in which there was so much that would have appealed to his peculiar artistic temperament.

The essay on Mr. Kenneth Grahame's famous book is remarkable as the only detailed tribute to the work of a generation younger than his own which Swinburne ever published. Generous sometimes to extravagance in his attitude to all predecessors and to some contemporaries, he did not willingly trust his judgment to weigh the qualities of his juniors. If, on the appearance of *The Golden Age* in 1895, he made an exception in favour of that masterpiece of delicate and penetrating humour, it was that he fell instantly and without resistance under the spell of its charm. Mr. Kenneth Grahame's picture of childhood appealed to Swinburne's intense delight in the company of little children, a foible which made him the idol of mothers and the laughing-stock of nurserymaids. He was never more radiantly happy than when passively enduring the tyranny of babes, and some of the most delightful recollections of him which we possess are connected with the infancy of our own little ones. I shall never lose from my memory the picture of the poet seated stiffly on the edge of the sofa (his favourite station) in our house in Delamere Terrace, with one of my small girls perched on each of his little knees, while my son, just advanced to knickerbockers, having climbed up behind him, with open palm was softly stroking his bald cranium, as though it had been the warm and delicious egg of some enormous bird. At that moment the rapturous face of the poet wore no trace of the "Olympian."

The reviews of *La Sieste de Jeanne* and of *Religions et Religion*, testify to the breathless and boundless admiration with which Swinburne regarded Victor Hugo at all times, but most passionately during the eight years of apotheosis which stretched from the publication of the new series of *La Legende des Siècles* (1877), to Victor Hugo's death (1885). Swinburne's attitude must strike most English readers as being one of almost insane extravagance, and in France itself the praise of Hugo has long ago shrunken between reasonable channels. But it must be remembered that in those years, to the majority of Frenchmen, Hugo appeared to be the greatest figure of the world; he was the authorised pontiff, almost the visible deity of literature. If the hyperboles of Swinburne seem excessive—and they not merely seem, but are excessive—let it be recollected that in those dazzling 'eighties, Renan could say that Victor Hugo had surpassed all the categories of literary history; Henri de Bornier that when Shakespeare had faded away in the extremity of time, Hugo would still be blazing; Léon Dierx that he sat on a throne above all the kings of the world. These were serious men, accustomed to severe expression, but the wind of Victor Hugo's old age blew upon them and maddened them, as it maddened the more susceptible Swinburne.

In 1886, the year after Hugo's death, Swinburne collected and arranged what at various times he had written, in *A Study of Victor Hugo*. From this he excluded all that we here reprint about *Religions et Religion*, probably because he felt it to be already out of proportion with the rest of his book. That series of poems, which was preceded by *Le Pape* and succeeded by *L'Âne*, received little attention even in 1880, in the midst of the apotheosis, and is in fact one of the most negligible of Hugo's works. The reader of it is stunned by the resounding rhetoric and the avalanche of high-sounding words, but is not rewarded by any of the poet's characteristic beauties.

At this moment, Victor Hugo was suffering, as someone said at the time, from the vertigo of his own celebrity. He had been so loudly told that he was impeccable and glorious and divine, that he thought he might pour out his melodious alexandrines at random. As M. Gaston Deschamps has said, "il fut victime de sa propre rhétorique, et tomba dans une phraséologie méchanique et automobile." It is a pity that Swinburne's excess of piety should have led him to praise this unhappy work in terms which suggest that he formed no conception of Hugo's error.

The fame of John Nichol was once considerable in academic circles, and his name will aways be connected with that of Swinburne, over whom he exercised a strong and not very beneficent authority. Four years Swinburne's senior, Nichol already occupied a prominent position at Balliol when Swinburne went up to Oxford in 1856, and Nichol encouraged him in his tastes for all the revolutionary forms of literature and politics. It was by Nichol that Swinburne was introduced to the society of the "Old Mortality," and the young Scotch don was the critic of the younger English poet's verses. In 1862 Nichol left Oxford to be appointed professor of English literature at Glasgow, a chair which he held for nearly thirty years. Henceforth Swinburne saw little of him, but he preserved a vivid sense of gratitude towards the man who had been almost the very first to recognise and foster Swinburne's genius. Nichol, with great learning and taste, had no genius at all, but unfortunately he believed himself to be a lyric and dramatic poet. When, in 1872, he published a perfectly unreadable *Hannibal* in blank verse, Swinburne was unable to escape from the task of reviewing it. The result may be read with amusement in its adroit avoidance of the difficulties. One feature which Swinburne did not note may be mentioned here. Nichol, advanced on all points, was a very early advocate of "votes for women," and in *Hannibal* he introduced his ideal of the "femme libre" in the personage of Fulvia, a prehistoric "Suffragette" who is something of an anachronism in Carthaginian society.

The long study of the work of Simeon Solomon (1840-1905) should be read in connection with that on *Les Fleurs du Mal*. It expresses more fully than any other portion of Swinburne's prose, the effect of Baudelaire's example upon his temperament. This essay was written in 1871, when he was much in the company of the brilliant young Jewish painter whose career was to be so tragic. Those who are acquainted only with the languid and ultra sentimental drawings of Simeon Solomon may be surprised to learn that he was extremely entertaining as a talker and even as a writer. He had the *vis comica* to a remarkable extent and he amused Swinburne as few other persons did. Rossetti said, on one occasion, quite indulgently, that Swinburne and Solomon had been romping about his studio like two boisterous children. Solomon was a very clever mimic, and he wrote vivacious sketches in skilful imitation of Dickens. In literature of a more serious kind, his only venture was the quarto, privately printed by F. S. Ellis in 1871, entitled *A Vision of Love revealed in Sleep : Until the Day break and the Shadows flee away.* Of this vague and visionary production, Swinburne gives a faithful account, scarcely biassed by friendship. After the catastrophe of 1873, Swinburne saw Simeon Solomon no more.

EDMUND GOSSE.

CONTENTS

	PAGE
INTRODUCTION	v
Les Fleurs du Mal	3
The Golden Age	19
La Sieste de Jeanne	31
Religions et Religion	41
The Well at the World's End	59
John Nichol's 'Hannibal'	65
Simeon Solomon: Notes on his 'Vision of Love,' and other Studies	75

LES FLEURS DU MAL

[*The Spectator*, September 6th, 1862.]

LES FLEURS DU MAL*

It is now some time since France has turned out any new poet of very high note or importance; the graceful, slight, and somewhat thin-spun classical work of M. Théodore de Banville hardly carries weight enough to tell across the Channel; indeed, the best of this writer's books, in spite of exquisite humorous character and a most flexible and brilliant style, is too thoroughly Parisian to bear transplanting at all. French poetry of the present date, taken at its highest, is not less effectually hampered by tradition and the taste of the greater number of readers than our own is. A French poet is expected to believe in philanthropy, and break off on occasion in the middle of his proper work to lend a shove forward to some theory of progress. The critical students there, as well as here, judging by the books they praise and the advice they proffer, seem to have pretty well forgotten that a poet's business is pre-

* *Les Fleurs du Mal*, par Charles Baudelaire. Édition augmentée de beaucoup de poèmes, et diminuée de six pièces. 1861.

sumably to write good verses, and by no means to redeem the age and remould society. No other form of art is so pestered with this impotent appetite for meddling in quite extraneous matters; but the mass of readers seem actually to think that a poem is the better for containing a moral lesson or assisting in a tangible and material good work. The courage and sense of a man who at such a time ventures to profess and act on the conviction that the art of poetry has absolutely nothing to do with didactic matter at all, are proof enough of the wise and serious manner in which he is likely to handle the materials of his art. From a critic who has put forward the just and sane view of this matter with a consistent eloquence, one may well expect to get as perfect and careful poetry as he can give.

To some English readers the name of M. Baudelaire may be known rather through his admirable translations, and the criticisms on American and English writers appended to these, and framing them in fit and sufficient commentary, than by his volume of poems, which, perhaps, has hardly yet had time to make its way among us. That it will in the long run fail of its meed of admiration, whether here or in France, we do not believe. Impeded at starting by a foolish and shameless prosecution, the first edition was, it appears, withdrawn before anything like a fair hearing had been obtained for it. The book now comes before us with a few of the original poems cancelled, but with important additions. Such as it now is, to sum up the merit and meaning of it is not easy to do in a few sentences. Like all good books, and all work of any original savour and strength, it will be long a debated point of argument, vehemently impugned and eagerly upheld.

We believe that M. Baudelaire's first publications were his essays on the contemporary art of France, written now many years since.* In these early writings there is already such admirable judgment, vigour of thought and style, and appreciative devotion to the subject, that the worth of his own future work in art might have been foretold even then. He has more delicate power of verse than almost any man living, after Victor Hugo, Browning, and (in his lyrics) Tennyson. The sound of his metres suggests colour and perfume. His perfect workmanship makes every subject admirable and respectable. Throughout the chief part of this book he has chosen to dwell mainly upon sad and strange things—the weariness of pain and the bitterness of pleasure—the perverse happiness and wayward sorrows of exceptional people. It has the languid, lurid beauty of close and threat-

* Salon de 1845 (1845); Salon de 1846 (1846). [ED.]

ening weather—a heavy, heated temperature, with dangerous hothouse scents in it; thick shadow of cloud about it, and fire of molten light. It is quite clear of all whining and windy lamentation; there is nothing of the bubbling and shrieking style long since exploded. The writer delights in problems, and has a natural leaning to obscure and sorrowful things. Failure and sorrow, next to physical beauty and perfection of sound or scent, seem to have an infinite attraction for him. In some points he resembles Keats, or still more his chosen favourite among modern poets, Edgar Poe; at times, too, his manner of thought has a relish of Marlowe, and even the sincerer side of Byron. From Théophile Gautier, to whom the book is dedicated, he has caught the habit of a faultless and studious simplicity; but, indeed, it seems merely natural to him always to use the right word and the right rhyme. How supremely musical and flexible a perfect artist in writing can make the French language, any chance page of the book is enough to prove; every description, the slightest and shortest even, has a special mark on it of the writer's keen and peculiar power. The style is sensuous and weighty; the sights seen are steeped most often in sad light and sullen colour.

As instances of M. Baudelaire's strength and beauty of manner, one might take especially the poems headed *Le Masque, Parfum Exotique La Chevelure, Les Sept Vieillards, Les Petites Vieilles, Brumes et Pluies ;* of his perfect mastery in description, and sharp individual drawing of character and form, the following stray verses plucked out at random may stand for a specimen :—

> *Sur ta chevelure profonde*
> *Aux âcres parfums,*
> *Mer odorante et vagabonde*
> *Aux flots bleus et bruns,*
>
> *Comme un navire qui s'eveille*
> *Au vent du matin,*
> *Mon âme rêveuse appareille*
> *Pour un ciel lointain.*
>
> *Tes yeux où rien ne se révèle*
> *De doux ni d'amer,*
> *Sont deux bijoux froids où se mêle*
> *L'or avec le fer.*
>
> *   *   *
>
> *Et ton corps se penche et s'allonge*
> *Comme un fin vaisseau*
> *Qui roule bord sur bord et plonge*
> *Ses vergues dans l'eau.*

The whole poem* is worth study for its vigorous beauty and the careful facility of its expression. Perhaps, though, the sonnet headed *Causerie* is a still completer specimen of the author's power. The way in which the sound and sense are suddenly broken off and shifted, four lines from the end, is wonderful for

* *Le Serpent qui danse.* [ED.]

effect and success. M. Baudelaire's mastery of the sonnet-form is worth remarking as a test of his natural bias towards such forms of verse as are most nearly capable of perfection. In a book of this sort, such a leaning of the writer's mind is almost necessary. The matters treated of will bear no rough or hasty handling. Only supreme excellence of words will suffice to grapple with and fitly render the effects of such material. Not the luxuries of pleasure in their simple first form, but the sharp and cruel enjoyments of pain, the acrid relish of suffering felt or inflicted, the sides on which nature looks unnatural, go to make up the stuff and substance of this poetry. Very good material they make too; but evidently such things are unfit for rapid or careless treatment. The main charm of the book is, upon the whole, that nothing is wrongly given, nothing capable of being re-written or improved on its own ground. Concede the starting point, and you cannot have a better runner.

Thus, even of the loathsomest bodily putrescence and decay, he can make some noble use; pluck out its meaning and secret, even its beauty, in a certain way, from actual carrion; as here, of the flies bred in a carcase:—

> *Tout cela descendait, montait comme une vague,*
> *Ou s'élançait en pétillant ;*
> *On eût dit que le corps, enflé d'un souffle vague,*
> *Vivait en se multipliant.*

Et ce monde rendait une étrange musique,
 Comme l'eau courante et le vent,
Ou le grain qu'un vanneur d'un mouvement rhythmique
 Agite et tourne dans son van.

Another of this poet's noblest sonnets is that *A une Passante*, comparable with a similar one of Keats, *Time's sea hath been five years at its slow ebb*, but superior for directness of point and forcible reality. Here for once the beauty of a poem is rather passionate than sensuous. Compare the delicate emblematic manner in which Keats winds up his sonnet with this sharp perfect finale :—

 Fugitive beauté
Dont le regard m'a fait soudainement renaître,
Ne te verrai-je plus que dans l'éternité ?
Ailleurs, bien loin d'ici, trop tard ! jamais peut-être !
Car j'ignore où tu fuis, tu ne sais où je vais,
Ô toi que j'eusse aimée, ô toi qui le savais !

There is noticeable also in M. Baudelaire's work a quality of *drawing* which recalls the exquisite power in the same way of great French artists now living. His studies are admirable for truth and grace; his figure-painting has the ease and strength, the trained skill, the beautiful gentle justice of manner, which come out in such pictures as *La Source* of Ingres, or that other splendid study of Flandrin, of a curled-up naked figure under full soft hot light, now exhibiting here. These verses of Baudelaire's are as perfect and good as either :—

> *Tes sourcils méchants*
> *Te donnent un air étrange,*
> *Qui n'est pas celui d'un ange,*
> *Sorcière aux yeux alléchants.*
> * * * *
> *Sur ta chair le parfum rôde*
> *Comme autour d'un encensoir ;*
> *Tu charmes comme le soir,*
> *Nymphe ténébreuse et chaude.*
> * * * *
> *Le désert et la forêt*
> *Embaument tes tresses rudes ;*
> *Ta tête a les attitudes*
> *De l'énigme et du secret ;*
>
> *Tes hanches sont amoureuses*
> *De ton dos et de tes seins,*
> *Et tu ravis les coussins*
> *Par tes poses langoureuses.*

Nothing can beat that as a piece of beautiful drawing.

It may be worth while to say something of the moral and meaning of many among these poems. Certain critics, who will insist on going into this matter, each man as deep as his small leaden plummet will reach, have discovered what they call a paganism on the spiritual side of the author's tone of thought. Stripped of its coating of jargon, this may mean that the poet spoken of endeavours to look at most things with the eye of an old-world poet; that he aims at regaining the clear and simple view of writers content to believe in the beauty of material subjects. To us, if this were the meaning of these people, we must say it seems a foolish one; for there is not one of these poems that could have been written in a time when it was not the fashion to dig for moral motives and conscious reasons. Poe, for example, has written poems without any moral meaning at all; there is not one poem of the *Fleurs du Mal* which has not a distinct and vivid background of morality to it. Only this moral side of the book is not thrust forward in the foolish and repulsive manner of a half-taught artist; the background, as we called it, is not out of drawing.

If any reader could extract from any poem a positive spiritual medicine—if he could swallow a sonnet like a moral prescription—then clearly the poet supplying these intellectual drugs would be a bad artist; indeed, no real artist, but a huckster and vendor of miscellaneous wares. But those who will look for them, may find moralities in plenty behind every poem of M. Baudelaire's; such poems especially as *Une Martyre*. Like a mediæval preacher, when he has drawn the heathen love, he puts sin on its right hand, and death on its left. It is not his or any artist's business to warn against evil; but certainly he does not exhort to it, knowing well enough that the one fault is as great as the other.

But into all this we do not advise any one to enter who can possibly keep out of it. When a book has been so violently debated over, so hauled this way and that by contentious critics, the one intent on finding that it means something mischievous, and the other intent on finding that it means something useful, those who are in search neither of a poisonous compound nor of a cathartic drug, had better leave the disputants alone, or take only such notice of them as he absolutely must take. Allegory is the dullest game and the most profitless taskwork imaginable: but if so minded a reader might extract most elaborate meanings between the Muse of the writer and that strange figure of a beautiful body with the head severed, laid apart

Sur la table de nuit comme une renoncule.

The heavy "mass of dark mane and heaps of precious jewels" might mean the glorious style and decorative language clothing this poetry of strange disease and sin; the hideous violence wrought by a shameless and senseless love might stand as an emblem of that analysis of things monstrous and sorrowful, which stamps the whole book with its special character. Then again, the divorce between all aspiration and its results might be here once more given in type; the old question re-handled:—

What hand and brain went ever paired?
What heart alike conceived and dared?

and the sorrowful final divorce of will from deed accomplished at last by force; and the whole thing summed up in that noble last stanza :—

Ton époux court le monde, et ta forme immortelle
Veille près de lui quand il dort ;
Autant que toi sans doute il te sera fidèle,
Et constant jusques à la mort.

All this and more might be worked out if the reader cared to try; but we hope he would not. The poem is quite beautiful and valuable enough as merely the " design of an unknown master." In the same way one might use up half the poems in the book; for instance, those three beautiful studies of cats (fitly placed in a book that has altogether a feline style of beauty — subtle, luxurious, with sheathed claws); or such carefully tender sketches as *Le Beau Navire*; or that Latin hymn " Franciscæ meæ laudes :—"

Novis te cantabo chordis,
O novelletum quod ludis
In solitudine cordis.

Esto sertis implicata,
O fœmina delicata
Per quam solvuntur peccata!

Some few indeed, as that *ex-voto* poem *A une Madone*, appeal at once to the reader as to an interpreter; they are distinctly of a mystical moral turn, and in that rich symbolic manner almost unsurpassable for beauty :—

> *Avec mes Vers polis, treillis d'un pur metal*
> *Savamment constellé de rimes de cristal,*
> *Je ferai pour ta tête une énorme Couronne ;*
> *Et dans ma Jalousie, ô mortelle Madone,*
> *Je saurai te tailler un Manteau, de façon*
> *Barbare, roide et lourd, et doublé de soupçon,*
> *Qui comme une guérite enfermera tes charmes ;*
> *Non de Perles brodé, mais de toutes mes Larmes !*
> *Ta Robe, ce sera mon Désir, frémissant,*
> *Onduleux, mon Désir qui monte et qui descend,*
> *Aux pointes se balance, aux vallons se repose,*
> *Et revêt d'un baiser tout ton corps blanc et rose.*

Before passing on to the last poem we wish to indicate for especial remark, we may note a few others in which this singular strength of finished writing is most evident. Such are, for instance, *Le Cygne, Le Poison, Tristesses de la Lune, Remords Posthume, Le Flacon, Ciel Brouillé, Une Mendiante Rousse* (a simpler study than usual, of great beauty in all ways, noticeable for its revival of the old fashion of unmixed masculine rhymes), *Le Balcon, Allegorie, L'Amour et le Crâne*, and the two splendid sonnets marked xxvii and xlii. We cite these headings in no sort of order, merely as they catch one's eye in revising the list of contents and recall the poems classed there. Each of them we regard as worth a separate study, but the *Litanies de Satan*, as in a way the key-note to this whole complicated tune of poems we had set aside for the last, much as (to judge by its place in the book) the author himself seems to have done.

Here it seems as if all failure and sorrow on earth, and all the cast-out things of the world—ruined bodies and souls diseased—made their appeal, in default of help, to Him in whom all sorrow and all failure were incarnate. As a poem, it is one of the noblest lyrics ever written; the sound of it between wailing and triumph, as it were the blast blown by the trumpets of a brave army in irretrievable retreat:—

> *O toi qui de la Mort, ta vieille et forte amante,*
> *Engendras l'Espérance—une folle charmante!*
> *O Satan, prends pitié de ma longue misère!*
>
> *Toi qui fais au proscrit ce regard calme et haut*
> *Qui damne tout un peuple autour d'un échafaud,*
> *O Satan, prends pitié de ma longue misère!*
>
> * * * *
>
> *Toi qui, magiquement, assouplis les vieux os*
> *De l'ivrogne attardé foulé par les chevaux,*
> *O Satan, prends pitié de ma longue misère!*
> *Toi qui, pour consoler l'homme frêle qui souffre,*
> *Nous appris à mêler le salpêtre et le soufre,*
> *O Satan, prends pitié de ma longue misère!*

These lines are not given as more finished than the rest; every verse has the vibration in it of naturally sound and pure metal. It is a study of metrical cadence throughout, of wonderful force and variety. Perhaps it may be best, without further attempts to praise or to explain the book, here to leave off, with its stately and passionate music fresh in our ears. We know that in time it must make its way; and to know when or how concerns us as little as it probably concerns the author, who can very well afford to wait without much impatience.

THE GOLDEN AGE

[*The Daily Chronicle*, March 31st, 1896].

THE GOLDEN AGE[*]

THE art of writing adequately and acceptably about children is among the rarest and most precious of all arts. Memory and observation, though these of course are necessary, are very far from sufficient to equip the student for such work. Inspiration is as much needed as even in the making of lyric verse; and since the deaths of George Eliot and Mrs. Ewing this peculiar inspiration had hitherto, as far as I know, been vouchsafed to none in such large and liberal measure as to Mrs. Molesworth; who surely should not condescend to lavish her time and her genius on grown-up people in their teens—or even older. That the place thus left vacant—the curule chair of infancy as represented and expounded by its chosen laureate or prophet—should have been taken by another woman, and worthily filled, would have been matter for delighted surprise: that it should be held by a man

[*] *The Golden Age*, by Kenneth Grahame.

is almost enough to redeem the reputation of his weaker and less perceptive sex. It is held by Mr. Kenneth Grahame: and he will not easily be unseated or supplanted. His *Golden Age* is one of the few books which are well-nigh too praiseworthy for praise. The fit reader—and the "fit" readers should be far from "few"—finds himself a child again while reading it. A child could only say what he liked and approved: and there is hardly a page in the volume for which the writer would not and should not get a good mark. The exceptionally excellent curate— exceptional among the "hopeless and incapable creatures" who had the stupid and sinful misfortune to be grown up—at once adds one to the number of our friends as soon as we meet him at the opening of the book, and find that he "would receive unblenching the information that the meadow beyond the orchard was a prairie studded with herds of buffalo, which it was our delight, moccasined and tomahawked, to ride down with those whoops that announce the scenting of blood. He neither laughed nor sneered, as the Olympians would have done; but possessed of a serious idiosyncrasy, he would contribute such lots of valuable suggestions as to the pursuit of this particular sort of big game that, as it seemed to us, his mature age and eminent position could scarce have been attained without a practical knowledge of the creature in its native lair. Then, too, he was always ready to constitute himself a possible army or a band of marauding Indians on the shortest possible notice—in brief, a distinctly able man, with talents, so far as we could judge, immensely above the majority. I trust he is a bishop by this time: he had all the necessary qualifications, as we knew."

The youngest reader or listener has his favourites among the characters that figure in the earliest stories he hears or reads: he is sure to prefer Achilles or Hector, Fitz James or Roderick Dhu. My favourite in this book is Harold—the "minimus." A more deliciously lifelike and original child was never begotten by fact or fancy. If it be permissible—but it hardly can be—to say so of any child, I should say that he would have been a good playfellow for Shakespeare's Mamillius. Speculation, wandering on ways reserved for the twin sciences of astrology and theology, may strive to reconstruct the stories they might have told each other, and the debates that might probably have followed. "There was a man dwelt by a churchyard"—Shakespeare's darling had time to tell his mother and us no more. But his tale, however infinitely more lovely and fanciful and attractive, could hardly have been more lifelike and childlike than this—and it is possible that Shakespeare, with his infinite love and knowledge of little as well as of elder children, would not have made it less derivative and more original:—

"I had just finished saying my prayers," began that young gentleman slowly, "when I happened to look out of the window, and on the lawn I saw a sight which froze the marrow in my veins! A burglar was approaching the house with snake-like tread! He had a scowl and a dark lantern, and he was armed to the teeth!"

We listened with interest. The style, though unlike Harold's native notes, seemed strangely familiar.

"Go on," said the curate grimly.

"Pausing in his stealthy career," continued Harold, "he gave a low whistle. Instantly the signal was responded to, and from the adjacent shadows two more figures glided forth. The miscreants were both armed to the teeth."

"Excellent," said the curate; "proceed."

"The robber chief," pursued Harold, warming to his work, "joined his nefarious comrades, and conversed with them in silent tones. His expression was truly ferocious, and I ought to have said that he was armed to the t——"

"There, never mind his teeth," interrupted the curate rudely; "there's too much jaw about you altogether. Hurry up and have done."

"I was in a frightful funk," continued the narrator, warily guarding his ear with his hand, "but just then the drawing-room window opened, and you and Aunt Maria came out—I mean emerged. The burglars vanished silently into the laurels, with horrid implications!"

The curate looked slightly puzzled. The tale was well sustained, and certainly circumstantial. After all, the boy might have really seen something. How was the poor man to know—though the chaste and lofty diction might have supplied a hint—that the whole yarn was a free adaptation from the last penny dreadful lent us by the knife-and-boot boy?

"Why did you not alarm the house?" he asked.

THE GOLDEN AGE

"'Cos I was afraid," said Harold, sweetly, "that p'r'aps they mightn't believe me!"

Immortality should be the reward—but it must have been the birthright—of the happy genius which perceived the burglars vanishing silently with horrid implications. And yet this passage is not more admirable in the fascination of its fidelity than the speculative discourse of little boys as to the subjects of conversation between little girls.

The prose epic of the Argonauts is attractive, but the humble adult who pens these diffident lines would much have preferred—not only for the sake of the childish reader—that the otherwise delightful and excellent Medea should not have dropped into poetry or pathos about an absent lover while talking to children. Does not some one of our contemporary foreign Shakespeares say, "People don't do such things"? and does not Echo answer, "I should rather hope not"?

But when the reader opens "the secret drawer" he must be a pitiable animal or vegetable if he does not enjoy his experience. The little fellow who "did want money so badly" has no notion, let his elders and inferiors observe, of pilfering or purloining what adventure may bestow on the adventurer. And "the list of demands" on his penniless purse is enough to turn a Herod into a Hugo. Such company

—the best of all good company—as we have been keeping throughout this book must surely make even the reader who may have the misfortune to move in society appreciate and sympathise with the ensuing reminiscences and reflections :—

> "I don't like society people," put in Harold from the sofa, where he was sprawling at full length—a sight the daylight hours would have blushed to witness. "There were some of 'em here this afternoon, when you two had gone off to the station. Oh, and I found a dead mouse on the lawn, and I wanted to skin it, but I wasn't sure I knew how, by myself; and they came out into the garden and patted my head—I wish people wouldn't do that—and one of 'em asked me to pick her a flower. Don't know why she couldn't pick it herself; but I said, 'All right, I will if you'll hold my mouse.' But she screamed and threw it away; and Augustine (the cat) got it, and ran away with it. I believe it was really his mouse all the time, 'cos he'd been looking about as if he had lost something, so I wasn't angry with *him;* but what did *she* want to throw away my mouse for?"
>
> "You have to be careful with mice," reflected Edward; "they're such slippery things. Do you remember we were playing with a dead mouse once on the piano, and the mouse was Robinson Crusoe, and the piano was the island, and somehow Crusoe slipped down inside the island, into its works, and we couldn't get him out, though we tried rakes and all sorts of things, till the tuner came. And that wasn't till a week after, and then——"

The setting of these jewels is necessary to give them their full and due relief; but it is no reviewer's business to transcribe a whole book. And yet the episode of "A Falling Out" can hardly be appreciated by stray samples of its pervasive and perfect charm. That it must be read as a whole, these extracts may suffice to show:—

Harold told me the main facts of this episode some time later in bits, and with reluctance. It was not a recollection he cared to talk about. The crude blank misery of a moment is apt to leave a dull bruise which is slow to depart, if it ever does so entirely; and Harold confesses to a twinge or two still, at times, like the veteran who brings home a bullet inside him from martial plains over sea.

He knew he was a brute the moment he had done it; Selina had not meant to worry, only to comfort and assist. But his soul was one raw sore within him, when he found himself shut up in the schoolroom after hours, merely for insisting that seven times seven amounted to forty-seven. The injustice of it seemed so flagrant. Why not forty-seven as much as forty-nine? The number was no prettier than the other to look at, and it was evidently only a matter of arbitrary taste and preference, and, anyhow, it had always been forty-seven to him, and would be to the end of time. So when Selina came in out of the sun, leaving the Trappers of the Far West behind her, and putting off the glory of being an Apaché squaw in order to hear him his tables and win his release, Harold turned on her venomously, rejected her kindly overtures, and even drove his elbow into her sympathetic ribs in his determination to be left alone in the glory of sulks. The fit passed directly, his eyes were opened, and his soul sat in the dust as he sorrowfully began to cast about for some atonement heroic enough to salve the wrong. Of course poor Selina looked for no sacrifice nor heroics whatever; she didn't even want him to say he was sorry. If he would only make it up she would have done the apologising part herself. But that was not a boy's way. Something solid Harold felt was due from him; and until it was achieved making up must not be thought of, in order that the final effect might not be spoilt. Accordingly, when his release came, and poor Selina hung about trying to catch his eye—Harold, possessed by the demon of a distorted motive, avoided her steadily—though he was bleeding inwardly at every minute of delay—and came to me instead. Needless to say, I approved his plan highly; it was so much more high-toned than just going and making up tamely, which anyone could do; and a girl who had been jobbed in the ribs by a hostile elbow could not be expected for a moment to overlook it, without the liniment of an offering to soothe her injured feelings.

"I know what she wants most," said Harold. "She wants that set of tea-things in the toy-shop window, with the red and blue flowers on 'em; she's wanted it for months, 'cos her dolls are getting big enough to have real afternoon tea, and she wants it so badly that she won't walk that side of the street when we go into the town. But it costs five shillings!"

Then we set to work seriously, and devoted the afternoon to a realisation of assets and the composition of a Budget that might have been dated, without shame, Whitehall.

Harold reached the town—so he recounted afterwards—in record time, having run most of the way for fear the tea-things, which had reposed six months in the window, should be snapped up by some other conscious-stricken lacerator of a sister's feelings; and it seemed hardly credible to find them still there, and their owner willing to part with them for the price marked on the ticket. He paid his money down at once, that there should be no drawing back from the bargain; and then, as the things had to be taken out of the window and packed, and the afternoon was yet young, he thought he might treat himself to a taste of urban joys and *la vie de Bohême*. Shops came first, of course, and he flattened his nose successively against the window with the indiarubber balls in it, and the clockwork locomotive; and against the barber's window, with wigs on blocks, reminding him of uncle's, and shaving cream that looked so good to eat; and the grocer's window, displaying more currants than the whole British population could possibly consume without a special effort; and the window of the bank, wherein gold was thought so little of that it was dealt about in shovels. Next there was the market-place, with all its clamorous joys; and when a runaway calf came down the street like a cannon-ball, Harold felt that he had not lived in vain. The whole place was so brimful of excitement that he had quite forgotten the why and the wherefore of his being there, when a sight of the church clock recalled him to his better self, and sent him flying out of the town, as he realised he had only just time enough left to get back in. If he were after his appointed hour, he would not only miss his high triumph, but probably would be detected as a transgressor of bounds—a crime before which a private opinion of multiplication sank to nothingness. So he jogged along on his homeward way, thinking of many things, and probably talking to himself a good deal, as his habit was, and covered nearly half the distance, when suddenly—a deadly sinking in the pit of his stomach—a paralysis of every limb—around him a world extinct of light and music—a black sun and a reeling sky —he had forgotten the tea-things!

Praise would be as superfluous as analysis would be impertinent. If others think otherwise, I can only say, in the words of the best and wisest of women who ever was underpaid at any price "They are born so, and will please themselves."

LA SIESTE DE JEANNE

[*The Athenæum*, February 24th, 1877.]

LA SIESTE DE JEANNE *

If among the treasures and wonders unearthed on the site of Mycenæ by the prosperous devotion and fortunate energy of Dr. Schliemann there had been found, in place of some ornament wrought of mere material ore, such a far costlier relic as one of those described by the living leader of English poets, in a phrase exquisite enough even for the priceless matter in hand; if the noble and happy labour of the now illustrious German could have been crowned by the discovery of something yet "more golden than very gold," more precious and marvellous than even such old-world miracles of carven metal as indeed have repaid it; if his research had glorified the world by the gift of a fresh addition to our too scanty treasure-house of

> *jewels five-words-long,*
> *That on the stretched forefinger of all time*
> *Sparkle for ever;*

---

* *La Sieste de Jeanne*, by Victor Hugo.

in that yet happier case, we cannot doubt that all who cherish the supreme art of speech transfigured into song would have marked the year 1876 as with a white pebble in the note-book of their memories. And if a jewel of such price was in effect thrown into that year's treasury—as unquestionably it has been— it would seem somewhat less than rational or gracious to take the less heed of it because it bears the image and superscription of no Greek demigod, but of an immortal who has not yet put off mortality; as surely he need not do to establish his claim to godhead by right of godlike glory and by proof of divine beneficence.

In the first week of November, 1876, the *République des Lettres* published a poem of just thirty-eight lines, *La Sieste de Jeanne*, every word of which, if any speech or memory of man endure so long, will be treasured as tenderly by generations as remote from the writer's as now treasure up with thankful wonder and reverence every golden fragment and jewelled spar from the wreck of Simonides or of Sappho. It has all the subtle tenderness, the spiritual fragrance as of a mother or a God, which invests the immortal song of Danaë; and the union of perfect grace with living passion, as it were the suffusion of human flesh and blood with heavenly breath and fire, brings back once again upon our thoughts the name which is above every name in lyric song. There is not one line which could have been written and set where it stands by the hand of any lesser than the greatest among poets. For once even the high priest and even the high priestess of baby-worship who have made their names immortal among our own by this especial and most gracious attribute—even William Blake and Christina Rossetti for once are distanced in the race of child-consecrated song, on their own sweet ground, across their own peculiar field of Paradise. Not even in the pastures that heard his pipe keep time to the *Songs of Innocence*, or on the "wet bird-haunted English lawn" set ringing as from nursery windows at summer sunrise to the faultless joyous music and pealing bird-like laughter of her divine *Sing-Song*, has there sounded quite such a note as this from the heaven of heavens in which little babies are adored by great poets, the frailest by the most potent of divine and human kind. Shakespeare and Landor each did more than once a good stroke of work in the divine service of young children; it is only out of the strong that such sweetness can come forth; only from the mouths of lions, not dead but living, that such honey can ever be distilled. And above the work in this lovely line of all poets in all time but one, there sits and smiles eternally the adorable baby who helps us for ever to forget all passing perversities of Christianized socialism or bastard Cæsarism which disfigure and disminish the pure proportions and the noble charm of *Aurora Leigh*. Even the most worshipful children born to art in Florence, and begotten upon stone or canvas by Andrea del Sarto or by Luca della Robbia's very self, must yield to that one the crown of sinless empire and the palm of powerless godhead which attest the natural mystery of their omnipotence; and which haply may help to explain why no accumulated abominations of cruelty and absurdity which inlay the record of its history and incrust the fabric of its creed can utterly corrode the natal beauty or corrupt the primal charm of a faith which centres at its opening round the worship of a new-born child.

The most accurate and affectionate description that I ever saw or heard given of a baby's incomparable smile, when graciously pleased to permit with courtesy and accept with kindness the votive touch of a reverential finger on its august little cheek, was given long since in the text accompanying a rich and joyous design of childish revel by Mr. Doyle; in which, if I rightly remember, a baby in arms was contemplating the riotous delights of its elders, fallen indeed from the sovereign state of infancy, but not yet degenerate into the lower life of adults, with that bland and tacit air of a large-minded and godlike tolerance which the devout observer will not fail to have remarked in the aspect of babies when unvexed and unincensed by any cross accident or any human shortcoming on the part of their attendant ministers. Possibly a hand which could paint that inexpressible smile might not fail also of the ability to render in mere words some sense of the ineffable quality which rests upon every line and syllable of this most divine poem. But, as it is, the best of us must be content to accept and absorb the perception of its heavenly beauty in that mood of helpless rapture which trembles between laughter and tears, suspended as it were for one sweet miraculous minute on the edge of a blind delight which divides till it combines them in a passionate confusion of their kinds. There are lines in it—but after all this is but an indirect way of saying that it is a poem by Victor Hugo—which may be taken as tests of the uttermost beauty, the extreme perfection, the supreme capacity and charm, to which the language of men can attain. As this:—

*Ses beaux petits pieds nus dont le pas est peu sûr
Dorment:*

a verse beyond all comment of articulate praise or thanksgiving. I was not minded to pluck out any petal from this paradisal rose by way of sample; but, having once put hand to it, I must needs take heart to touch yet another leaf of its central and crowning glories.

> *Donc, à l'heure où les feux du soleil sont calmants,*
> *Quand toute la nature écoute et se recueille,*
> *Vers midi, quand les nids se taisent, quand la feuille*
> *La plus tremblante oublie un instant de frémir,*
> *Jeanne a cette habitude aimable de dormir.*

It might seem as if the Fates could not allow two men capable of such work in one line as that to live together in one time of the world; and that Shelley therefore had to die in his thirtieth year as soon as Hugo had attained his twentieth. I dare cite but one couplet more; for what follows is too ineffably and adorably beautiful to permit another pause before the perfect end:—

> *On la contemple, on rit, on sent fuir la tristesse,*
> *Et c'est un astre, ayant de plus la petitesse.*

If the last word on so divine a subject could ever be said, it surely might well be none other than this. But with workmen of the very highest order there is no such thing as a final touch, a point at which they like others are compelled to draw bridle, a summit on which even their genius also may abide but while a man takes breath, and halt without a hope or aspiration to pass beyond it. Were it not that the Master has a hundred and a thousand times in his life convinced us (half reluctant) of this truth, and confuted all possible conceit or surmise on our part that now at least here at last must be the limit of all triumph, beyond all reach or dream or vision of all the lesser sons of men, which could even for him be conceivable; were it not that by this time we should all know better, we might now if ever claim pardon or plead excuse for the vain and hazardous assumption; but in face of the untraversed and unsounded sea of song on whose shore we stand even now expectant of the magic argosies to come, and count the very hours as they lessen which bring us closer to the day when we shall have actually in hand the second issue of the *Légende des Siècles*, we can but possess our souls in impatience and expect what heaven will send us at our Master's inexhaustible and immortal hand.

Note.—Some paragraphs excerpted from this Review were embodied in *A Study of Victor Hugo*, 1886, pp. 82-85.

RELIGIONS ET RELIGION

[*The Fortnightly Review*, June, 1880.]

RELIGIONS ET RELIGION [*]

IF the sense of stupefaction could become one with the sense of rapture, and find for itself utterance or make for itself expression in words where judicial comment should be summed up and swallowed up in spiritual thanksgiving, this would be the mood and this the method in which, if in any, we might without overmuch misgiving undertake at the present date to approach the work and the name of Victor Hugo. I at least think it well to introduce the little I can hope to say on the matter by this avowal of imbecility and incompetence to do much more than "wonder with a foolish face of praise"; by a plain and simple confession and profession of contented inadequacy and satisfied inability to revise and correct the doings and designs of our dearest and most mighty master, "with an austere regard of control" such as might beseem the gravity of

[*] *Religions et Religion*, by Victor Hugo, 1880.

Malvolio or the more malevolent Sainte-Beuvre. It is for my elders and precursors in criticism as in poetry to appeal, if they will, on this subject, from the judgment of the world to the judgment of Weimar; worth exactly and accurately as much as the final verdict of Ferney on the cognate subject of Shakespeare. It is for me and such as I am to salute in silence or in speech one of the most glorious wonders that ever the world has witnessed: the triumph at seventy-eight of a greater warrior and a more venturesome seafarer than Dandolo at ninety-seven. Of our fleet also, who follow in his wake with our smaller craft of prose or verse, the lord high admiral is a Republican who leads us, over stormier seas than the Adriatic, to a brighter goal than Byzantium. But there is one unmistakable point of most happy difference: our foremost seaman is very far otherwise than blind.

"This book," he tells us, "was begun in 1870; it is finished in 1880. The year 1870 gave infallibility to the Pope and Sedan to the Empire. What will the year 1880 do?" Rather than hazard a conjecture on that point, we may reflect on what the greatest man in our present world has given for all time to all mankind since France shook off the venomous beast of Empire into the fatal fire of rekindled war, and Badinguet slunk forth to rot alive and dead in the appropriate shades of Chislehurst. In these ten years he has given us of poetry alone enough whereon to found the fame of ten poets. The second series of the *Légende des Siècles*, a gift too vast in its magnificence for the measure of human thanksgiving : *L'Art d'être Grand-père*, a gift too precious in its loveliness for estimate of human speech : *Le Pape*, a vision of Christ evoked before Christendom, more sweet than the sweetest music, more bitter than the bitterest tears : *La Pitié Suprême*, the very final note of heavenly mercy made manifest in divinity of wisdom and vocal through tenderness of truth. And all his gifts are given with such large and liberal ease of hand that he seems to offer and we are tempted to accept them as leaves from a tree, or fragrance from a flower, or water from a wellspring, or sunlight from the sun : we come indeed by inevitable habit to consider him in the end as no poet of our own human kind, though he love man well enough to bring us again from heaven the fire of everlasting life : no priest on earth of the sun-God, but the very sun of heaven itself made human in a poet as of old.

For the very shadow of this man's presence is a sunbeam of the very light indeed, and for every year that he lives there is because of him less darkness in the world. Nor ever before this has his light been turned upon a darker place than now that it is flashed full upon the creeds of human faith. The poem called *Religions et Religion* is throughout an impeachment of all mere materialism; and first and foremost of the worst existing or surviving form of materialism in the whole world. A creed which is based on deicide and sustained on theophagy is never more insupportably laughable or more laughably insupportable than when its advocates denounce or deride their antagonists as—of all opprobrious names upon earth—materialists. The men of our own day are far indeed from being the first to remark on the incomparable drollery of such a term of reproach from lips which profess belief in the mortality of an immortal, in the interruption of an eternity; but no thinker or reasoner of the past ever brought heavier or sharper weapons from the armoury of reason to the panoply of truth to bear upon the monstrous and murderous absurdities of his day than here has Victor Hugo in our own. But even Cardinal Newman's *Grammar of Assent* is not a more powerful protest in favour of sheer atheistic nihilism than is this book on behalf of the opposite creed; of revival or survival, continuity or advance in the individual existence and conscious personality of the human spirit. As all the pleading and reasoning powers of his most eloquent Eminence in that most memorable argument were lavished on demonstration of the fact or circulation of the fallacy that there is no sure refuge from the pelting storm of nihilistic dogmatism but in the bosom of a deicidal and theophagous Christianity, so here are all the reasoning and pleading powers of a greater than he girt up to deny and to disprove it. Many a student, if I may presume to argue from one single insignificant instance, might say to the great theologian—Almost thou persuadest me to be a nihilist; to the great free-thinker—Almost thou persuadest me to be a believer in the sure and certain immortality of the personal and individual soul.

The direct aim of this book is rather to refute the converse than the obverse of the proposition advanced by the Catholic theosophist; to answer those who contend that positive nihilism or nihilistic positivism is inevitable if Christianity as expressed in its creeds and embodied in its sacraments be incredible, than those who argue that if dogmatic nihilism be indigestible we are bound to swallow the alternative prescription of clerical and sacramental Christianity. Singular as it may seem to certain philo-Christian disbelievers in the Catholic faith, it would hardly appear to have occurred to the bemused intelligence and limited imagination of this too presumptuous poet, that Judaism may consist or coexist with disbelief in the Creeds, or Mahometanism with disbelief in the Koran. For him, therefore, the whole question is whether there be not—as he for one is assured that there must be—an escape from the dilemma presented and obtruded by these two long-horned and sharp-edged alternatives—Christianity is certainly true, or no faith certainly is credible: on the one horn Büchner is impaled, and Newman on the other; Pascal, one might add, in a perpetual alternation of torments, is successively impaled on both. Four principles of thought, we may say, are here impeached and impugned: a double enemy is assailed by the lover of faith and reason, love and hope, in the militant materialism of Papists and Positivists; by the lover of justice and mercy, humanity and freedom, in the Catholic philosophy of de Maistre and the Calvinistic misosophy of Carlyle. And if the sarcasms on theology seem to any reader more keen and violent than the satire on any other form of unbelief or infidelity to the truth as here conceived, he should remember that superstition with a lining of materialism is surely a worse thing than materialism stark naked; and that while it is palpably possible to be a materialist without being a Christian, it is implicitly impossible to be a Christian without being a materialist.

As a sample of what we may call the first manner of this poem, we may take the following explicit and exhaustive summary of truths generally necessary to salvation.

Vous prêtez au bon Dieu ce raisonnement-ci :

> —*J'ai, jadis, dans un lieu charmant et bien choisi*
> *Mis la première femme avec le premier homme ;*
> *Ils ont mangé, malgré ma défense, une pomme ;*
> *C'est pourquoi je punis les hommes à jamais.*
> *Je les fais malheureux sur terre, et leur promets*
> *En enfer, où Satan dans la braise se vautre,*
> *Un châtiment sans fin pour la faute d'un autre.*
> *Leur âme tombe en flamme et leur corps en charbon.*
> *Rien de plus juste. Mais, comme je suis très bon,*
> *Cela m'afflige. Hélas ! comment faire ? Une idée !*
> *Je vais leur envoyer mon fils dans la Judée ;*
> *Ils le tueront. Alors,—c'est pourquoi j'y consens,—*
> *Ayant commis un crime, ils seront innocents.*
> *Leur voyant ainsi faire une faute complète,*
> *Je leur pardonnerai celle qu'ils n'ont pas faite ;*
> *Ils étaient vertueux, je les rends criminels ;*
> *Donc je puis leur rouvrir mes vieux bras paternels,*
> *Et de cette façon cette race est sauvée,*
> *Leur innocence étant par un forfait lavée.*

Let us hear now the graver note of scientific or philosophic objection to the faith incarnate in the life and embodied in the teaching of Victor Hugo :—

> *Matière ou pur esprit, bloc sourd ou dieu sublime,*
> *Le monde, quel qu'il soit, c'est ce qui dans l'abîme*
> *N'a pas dû commencer et ne doit pas finir.*
> *Quelle prétention as-tu d'appartenir*
> *A l'unité suprême et d'en faire partie,*
> *Toi, fuite ! toi monade en naissant engloutie,*

Qui jettes sur le gouffre un regard insensé,
Et qui meurs quand le cri de ta vie est poussé!

Ah! triste Adam, flocon qui fonds presque avant d'être,
Lugubre humanité, n'est-ce pas trop de naître?
N'est-ce pas trop d'avoir à vivre, en vérité,
Ô morne genre humain, bref, rapide, emporté!
Il ne te suffit pas, quoique ta fange souffre,
D'apparaître une fois dans la lueur du gouffre!
L'homme éternel, voilà ce que l'homme comprend.
Tu demandes au ciel, au grand ciel ignorant
Qui t'assourdit de foudre et t'aveugle d'étoiles,
Quel fil te noue, ô mouche, à ses énormes toiles,
Comment il tient à l'homme, et quel est ce lien?
Tu devrais te sentir pourtant tellement rien
Qu'avec ce vil néant que tu nommes ta sphère
Le ciel—en supposant qu'il soit—n'a rien à faire!
Tout ce qu'il peut cacher, couver ou contenir,
Est hors de toi, qui n'as qu'un soir pour avenir.
Ô le risible effort de rattacher ce dôme
De prodige, d'horreur et d'ombre à ton atome!
Quel besoin as-tu donc d'être de l'univers?
Chair promise au tombeau, contente-toi des vers!

And, finally, let us refresh our very "spirit of sense" with a last deep draught of music from the closing anthem of a loftier liturgy than ever was chanted in any temple or cathedral where men worshipped otherwise than in spirit and in truth.

Vis, et fais ta journée; aime et fais ton sommeil.
Vois au-dessus de toi le firmament vermeil;
Regarde en toi ce ciel profond qu'on nomme l'âme;
Dans ce gouffre, au zénith, resplendit une flamme.

RELIGIONS ET RELIGION

Un centre de lumière inaccessible est là.
Hors de toi comme en toi cela brille et brilla ;
C'est là-bas, tout au fond, en haut du précipice.
Cette clarté toujours jeune, toujours propice,
Jamais ne s'interrompt et ne pâlit jamais ;
Elle sort des noirceurs, elle éclate aux sommets ;
La haine est de la nuit, l'ombre est de la colère !
Elle fait cette chose inouïe, elle éclaire.
Tu ne l'éteindrais pas si tu la blasphémais ;
Elle inspirait Orphée, elle échauffait Hermès ;
Elle est le formidable et tranquille prodige ;
L'oiseau l'a dans son nid, l'arbre l'a dans sa tige ;
Tout la possède, et rien ne pourrait la saisir ;
Elle s'offre immobile à l'éternel désir,
Et toujours se refuse et sans cesse se donne ;
C'est l'évidence énorme et simple qui pardonne ;
C'est l'inondation des rayons, s'épanchant
En astres dans un ciel, en roses dans un champ ;
C'est ici, là, partout, en haut, en bas, sans trêve,
Hier, aujourd'hui, demain, sur le fait, sur le rêve,
Sur le fourmillement des lueurs et des voix,
Sur tous les horizons de l'abîme à la fois,
Sur le firmament bleu, sur l'ombre inassouvie,
Sur l'être, le déluge immense de la vie !
C'est l'éblouissement auquel le regard croit.
De ce flamboiement naît le vrai, le bien, le droit ;
Il luit mystérieux dans un tourbillon d'astres ;
Les brumes, les noirceurs, les fléaux, les désastres
Fondent à sa chaleur démesurée, et tout
En sève, en joie, en gloire, en amour, se dissout :
S'il est des cœurs puissants, s'il est des âmes fermes,
Cela vient du torrent des souffles et des germes
Qui tombe à flots, jaillit, coule, et, de toutes parts,
Sort de ce feu vivant sur nos têtes épars.
Il est ! il est ! Regarde, âme. Il a son solstice,
La Conscience : il a son axe, la Justice ;
Il a son équinoxe, et c'est l'Égalité ;

E

*Il a sa vaste aurore, et c'est la Liberté.
Son rayon dore en nous ce que l'âme imagine.
Il est! il est! il est! sans fin, sans origine,
Sans éclipse, sans nuit, sans repos, sans sommeil.*

Renonce, ver de terre, à créer le soleil.

It is notorious to all imbeciles that a poet, being as it were a kind of musical box in breeches to be wound up now and then for a tune, cannot possibly be a theologian, politician, or philosopher, and it is not usually supposed that a philosopher, a politician or a theologian can (even if he would condescend to) be a poet; though to my own poor instinct it would seem that the illustrious author of the *Dream of Gerontius* is often a true and sometimes an exquisite singer. But as on these high matters my humble opinion must of necessity be worthless, it is full time that I should turn from investigation of the substance to remark on the style of this poem. And on this subject one bolder and more eloquent than I might well be baffled. To analyse the style of the greatest among writers would need the subtlety, to praise it would need the inspiration, of their own inaccessible genius. And for a commentator of foreign name, though not wholly alien either in blood or in affection from France, it might well seem even specially presumptuous to undertake a task in which the most competent and the best willing of

French critics could look only for a relative success. Thus baffled and belated on both sides, I prefer to seek refuge in brief quotation from one or two of the articles which have appeared on this poem in Parisian journals: taking first a word or two from the *Journal des Débats*.

"That a man should not admire the work of Victor Hugo is conceivable; a man may be born blind. But that any one should admire it with reservations is no longer intelligible. Do men make reservations in face of the immensity of the sea, the greatness of a mountain, the glory of the sun? For ourselves, when we read Victor Hugo, one only feeling possesses us—that of admiration. This admiration we feel for the master's entire work, from the verses of that twentieth year which was so full of hopes, to the verses of this magnificent old age which is so full of glory. Three quarters of a century have passed over this man without bowing his head, without making the flame of his genius flicker. Victor Hugo remains robust as is his work. He bids defiance to age as his work bids defiance to time. One would think, to see his face at once grave and smiling, and still so young under its aureole of white hair, that the poet has felt not the assault but the kiss of years."

No man is more averse than I from that impertinence of personal allusion or description which European journalism would do well if it would leave to the more shameless scribblers of America; but surely no man will find in this reverent and graceful reference to an obvious and most happy truth any lack of veneration or delicate respect.

The *France* remarks, in the teeth of all malevolent

affirmations to the contrary, on the absolutely loyal consistency and fidelity of Victor Hugo "to all his manly past." "Only, as he advances in age, the poet quintessentializes and *sublimates* his thought. He gives it the final form, precise and positive. Never has the verse of Victor Hugo been firmer and more supple. At one time it is all of a piece, and seems cast as it were in a single jet out of the fired imagination of the poet. At another time the verse, like the thought, folds itself back upon itself (*se replie*), breaks and meanders, and is but all the stronger and the more harmonious. In our humble opinion, never was the science of poetic speech carried further than in this book."

"This volume," says the *Télégraphe*, "begins with polemics, proceeds with research, winds up with affirmation. The first part would delight Voltaire; Jouffroy would not disown the second; and Swedenborg would not feel himself much "—Blake, we may add, would not feel himself at all—" out of his own line in the last. In this sense Victor Hugo is a complete thinker, a harmonious organization" ("that's a vile phrase," as Polonius has it, in English), "and this it is which accounts for his vigorous moral health, his vigorous and robust old age. The rationalist in him keeps on good terms with the mystic; and both agree in conceding to the sceptic that share which should honestly be granted him by the weakness of our intelligence and the insufficiency of our knowledge. —The rapid success of this book is a good symptom. The public must be beginning to weary of *Assommoirs* and *Nanas*" (heaven grant it may! for heaven knows it is high time), " since it can applaud the poet who opens for it an outlook on infinity."

But far above all these, and high above any poor effort of mine at any tolerable translation, hangs the golden tribute, suspended in a golden shrine, of Théodore de Banville. The most honey-tongued of poets, the Simonides Melicertes, the Tibullus or the Tennyson of France (with a stanchless vein in him of such pure and precious humour as reminds us almost of Aristophanes at its best), has laid upon our master's altar an offering of right royal price and of most loyal love. The transfusion of this classic œnomel into the vessels of a foreign tongue is only less difficult than tempting to the taster as a task.

He writes thus—or as nearly thus as I can render his writing—in the *National* :—

"In the midst of our confused life, turbulent and flat, bustling and indifferent, where books and plays, dreams and poems, driven down a wind of oblivion, are like the leaves which November sweeps away, and fly past, without giving us time to tell one from another, in a vague whirl and rush, at times there appears a new book by Victor Hugo, and everything lights up, resounds, murmurs, and sings at once.

"The shining, sounding, fascinating verse, with its thousand surprises of sound, of colour, of harmony, breaks forth like a rich concert, and ever newly stirred, dazzled and astonished, as if we were hearing verses for the first time, we remain stupefied with wonder before the persistent prodigy of the great seer, the great thinker, the unheard-of artist, self-transfigured without ceasing, always new and always like himself. It would be impertinent to say of him that he makes progress; and yet I find no other word to express the fact that every hour, every minute, he adds something new, something yet more exact and yet more caressing, to that swing of syllables, that melodious play of rhyme renascent of itself, which is the grace and the invincible power of French poetry"—if English ears could but learn or would but hear it; whereas usually they have never been taught even the rudiments of French prosody, and receive the most perfect cadences of the most glorious or the most exquisite French poetry as a schoolboy who has not yet learnt scansion might receive the melodies of Catullus or of Virgil.

"Let me be forgiven a seeming blasphemy; but since the time of periphrasis is over the real truth of things must be said of them. Well, then, the great peril of poetry is the risk it runs of becoming a weariness: for it may be almost sublime and yet perfectly wearisome: but, on the contrary, with all its bewildering flight, its vast circumference, and the rage of its genius grown drunk with things immeasurable, the poetry of Victor Hugo is of itself *amusing* into the bargain—amusing as a fairy tale, as a many-coloured festival, as a lawless and charming comedy; for in it words play unexpected parts, take on themselves a special and intense life, put on strange or graceful faces, clash one against another either cymbals of gold or urns of crystal, exchange flashes of living light and dawn.

"And let no one suspect in my choice of an epithet any idea of diminution: a garden-box on a window-sill may be thoroughly wearisome, and an immense forest may be amusing, with its shades wherein the nightingale sings, its giant trees with the blue sky showing through them, its mossy shelters where the silver brooklet hums its tune through the moistened greenery. Ay,—

this is one of its qualities,—the poetry of Hugo can be read, can be devoured as one devours a new novel, because it is varied, surprising, full of the unforeseen, clear of common-places, like nature itself; and of such a limpid clearness as to be within the reach of every creature who can read, even when it soars to the highest summits of philosophy and idealism. In fact, to be obscure, confused, unintelligible, is not a rare quality, nor one difficult to acquire ; and the first fool you may fall in with can easily attain to it. In this magnificent poem which has just appeared—as, for that matter, in all his other poems—what Victor Hugo does is just to dispel and scatter to the winds of heaven those lessons, those fogs, those rubbish-heaps, those clouds of dark bewildered words with which the sham wise men of all ages have overlaid the plain evidence of truth."

"The words of Mercury are harsh after the songs of Apollo"; and I, who cannot pretend even to the gift of eloquence proper to the son of Maia, will not presume to add a word of less valuable homage to the choicer tribute of Banville. But it may possibly not be as superfluous as assuredly it should be to remark that in his wittiest and keenest impeachment of Christianity the most Christlike of living poets neither expresses nor implies any contumelious animadversion on the divine humanity of the man once murdered by the malignity and ever since maligned by the adoration of priests.

THE WELL AT THE WORLD'S END

[*The Nineteenth Century*, November, 1896.]

THE WELL AT THE WORLD'S END *

THE creative gift of Mr. Morris, his distinctive power of imagination, cannot be defined or appreciated by any such test of critical comparison as is applicable to the work of any other man. He is himself alone, and so absolutely that his work can no more be likened to any mediæval than to any contemporary kinsman's. In his love of a story for a story's sake he is akin to Chaucer and the French precursors of Chaucer: but if he has not much of Chaucer's realistic humour and artistic power of condensation and composition, he has a gift of invention as far beyond Chaucer's as the scope of a story like *The Well at the World's End* is beyond the range of such brief romances as *Amis and Amile*, or *Aucassin and Nicolette*. Readers and lovers (the terms should here be synonymous) of his former tales or poems in prose will expect to find in this masterpiece—for a

* *The Well at the World's End*, by William Morris.

perfect and unique masterpiece it is—something that will remind them less of *Child Christopher* than of *The Wood beyond the World*. The mere likeness in the titles would suggest so much: and this I think they will not fail to find: but I am yet more certain that the quality of this work is even finer and stronger than that of either. The interest, for those who bring with them to the reading of a work of imagination any auxiliary or sympathetic imagination of their own, is deeper and more vivid as well as more various: but the crowning test and triumph of the author's genius will be recognised in the all but unique power of touching with natural pathos the alien element of magical or supernatural fiction. Coleridge could do this: who else till now has done it? And when we venture to bring in the unapproachable name of Coleridge, we are venturing to cite the example of the most imaginative, the most essentially poetic, among all poets of all nations and all time.

It should be remembered that when an allegorical intention was detected in the beautiful story of adventure and suffering and love which enchanted all readers in *The Wood beyond the World*, Mr. Morris for once condescended to disclaim the misinterpretation of his meaning, and to point out the difference between allegorical and simple narrative in words of perfect and conclusive accuracy. No commentator, I should hope, will ever waste his time on the childish task of inventing an occult significance for the incidents and adventures, the lurid and the lovely landscapes, set before him and impressed upon his memory in this later and yet more magically beautiful tale. The perfect simplicity and the supreme nobility of the spirit which informs and pervades and quickens and exalts it, must needs make any but an inept and incapable reader feel yet once more a sense of wonder at the stupidity of the generations which could imagine a difference and a contrast between simple and noble. The simplest English writer of our time is also the noblest: and the noblest by reason and by virtue of his sublime simplicity of spirit and of speech. If the English of the future are not utterly unworthy and irredeemably unmindful of the past, they will need no memorial to remind them that his name was William Morris.

JOHN NICHOL'S 'HANNIBAL'

[*The Fortnightly Review*, December, 1872.]

JOHN NICHOL'S 'HANNIBAL'*

The historic or epic drama, as perhaps we might more properly call it, is assuredly one of the hardest among the highest achievements of poetry. The mere scope or range of its aim is so vast, so various, so crossed and perplexed by diverse necessities and suggestions starting from different points of view, that the simple intellectual difficulty is enough to appal and repel any but the most laborious servants of the higher Muse; and to this is added the one supreme necessity of all—to vivify the whole mass of mere intellectual work with imaginative fire; to kindle and supple and invigorate with poetic blood and breath the inert limbs, the stark lips and empty veins of the naked subject: a task in which the sculptor who fails of himself to give his statue life will find no favouring god to help him by inspiration or infusion from without of an alien and miraculous vitality. In this case Pygmalion must look to himself

* *Hannibal: a Historical Drama.* By John Nichol.

for succour, and put his trust in no hand but his own.

There are two ways in which a poet may treat a historic subject: one, that of Marlowe and Shakespeare, in the fashion of a dramatic chronicle; one, that of the greatest of all later dramatists, who seizes on some point of historic tradition, some character or event proper or possible to the time chosen, be it actual or ideal, and starting from this point takes his way at his will, and from this seed or kernel develops as it were by evolution the whole fabric of his poem. It would be hard to say which method of treatment requires the higher and the rarer faculty; to throw into poetic form and imbue with dramatic spirit the whole body of an age, the whole character of a great event or epoch, by continuous reproduction of historic circumstance and exposition of the recorded argument scene by scene; or to carve out of the huge block of history and chronicle some detached group of ideal figures, and give them such form and colour of imaginative life as may seem best to you. In some of the greatest plays of Victor Hugo there is hardly more than a nominal connection perceptible at first sight with historical character or circumstance. In *Marion de Lorme*, Richelieu is an omnipresent shadow, a spectral omnipotence; Mary Tudor was never convicted before any tribunal but the poet's of any warmer weakness than the religious faith which had heat enough only to consume other lives than her own in other flames than those of illicit love; and Lucrezia Estense Borgia died peaceably in lawful childbed, in the fifteenth year of her fourth marriage. Nevertheless, these great works belong properly to the class of historical drama: they have in them the breath and spirit of the chosen age, and the life of their time informs the chosen types of ideal character. The Cromwell of Hugo, in his strength and weakness, his evil and his good, is as actual and credible a human figure as the Cromwell of Carlyle, whether or not we accept as probable or possible matter of historic fact the alloy of baser metal which we here see mingled with the fine gold of heroic intellect and action. He who can lay hold of truth need fear no charge of falsehood in his free dealing with mere fact; and this first play of Hugo's, in my mind the most wonderful intellectual production of any poet on record at the age of twenty-five, is with all its licence of invention and diversion of facts, an example throughout of perfect poetic truth and life.

It is to the former school—to the school founded, in his *Edward II.*, by the great father of English tragedy —that we have now to welcome the accession of a new and a worthy disciple. In this large and perilous field of work the labourers of any note or worth have been few indeed. Except for the one noble drama in which Ford has embodied a brief historic episode, the field has lain fallow from the age of Shakespeare to our own, and our own has produced but one workman equal to the task; for even the single attempt of Mr. Browning in the line of pure historic drama can hardly be counted as successful enough to rank with the master poem of Sir Henry Taylor. Nor indeed are we likely to see the work in this kind which for intellectual majesty and interest, for large and serene possession of character and event, for grasp and mastery of thought and action, may deserve to be matched against *Philip van Artevelde*. But it is to the same class of "chronicle history," to use the Shakespearian term of definition, that Mr. Nichol's drama of *Hannibal* must properly be assigned. The daring and magnitude of the design would alone suffice to make it worthy of note, even were the success accomplished less real than we find it to be. The man who attempts in an age of idyllic poetry to write a heroic poem, or to write a dramatic poem in an age of analytic verse, deserves at least the credit due to him who sees and knows the best and highest, and strives to follow after it with all his heart and might. For the higher school of intellectual poetry must always of its nature be dramatic and heroic; these are assuredly the highest and the best things of art, and not the delicacies or intricacies of the idyllic or the analytic school of writing. The two chief masters of song are the dramatist and the lyrist; and in the higher lyric as well as in the higher drama the note sounded must have in it something of epic or heroic breath.

But we find here much more than breadth of scheme or courage of design to praise. The main career of Hannibal down to the battle of the Metaurus is traced scene after scene in large and vigorous outline; and for the action and reaction of dramatic intrigue we have the simpler epic interest of the harmonious succession of great separate events. Throughout the exposition of this vast subject, as act upon act of that heroic and tragic poem, the life of one man weighed against the world and found all but able to overweigh it, is unrolled before us on the scroll of historic song, there is a high spirit and ardour of thought which sustains the scheme of the poet, and holds on steadily through all change of time and place, all diversity of incident and effect, toward the accomplishment of his general aim. The worth of a poem of this kind cannot of course be gauged by any choice of excerpts; if it could, that worth would be little indeed. For in this mixed kind of art something more and other than poetic fancy or even than high imagination is requisite for success; the prime necessity is that shaping force of intellect which can grasp and mould its subject without strain and without relaxation. This power of composition is here always notable. Simple as is the structure of a "chronicle history," it calls for no less exercise of this rare and noble gift than is needed for the manipulation of an elaborate plot or fiction. It is in this, the most important point of all, that we find the work done most deserving of our praise.

On a stage so vast and crowded in the scheme embracing so many years and agents, the greater number of the multitudinous actors who figure in turn before us cannot of course be expected to show any marked degree of elaboration in the outline of their various lineaments; but however slight or swift in handling, the touch of the draughtsman is never indistinct or feeble; Roman and Carthaginian, wise man and unwise, heroic and unheroic, pass each on his way with some recognisable and rememberable sign of identity. Upon one figure alone besides that of his hero the author has expended all his care and power. Of this one ideal character the conception is admirable, and worthy of the hand of a great poet; nor does the execution of the design fail, as it proceeds, to repay our hope and interest at starting. Here as elsewhere the requisite hurry of action and conflict of crowding circumstance forbid any subtle or elaborate analysis of detail; but in a few scenes and with a few strokes the figure of Fulvia stands

JOHN NICHOL'S 'HANNIBAL'

before us complete. From the slight and straggling traditions of Hannibal's luxurious entanglement in Capua, Mr. Nichol has taken occasion to create a fresh and memorable type of character, and give colour and variety to the austere and martial action of his poem by an episode of no inharmonious passion. To no vulgar "harlot" such as Pliny speaks of has he permitted his hero to bow down. The revolted Roman maiden who casts her life into the arms of her country's enemy is a mistress not unworthy of Hannibal. From the first fiery glimpse of her active and passionate spirit to the last cry of triumph which acclaims the consummation of her love in death, we find no default or flaw in the noble conception of her creator. At her coming into the poem

> "*She makes a golden tumult in the house
> Like morning on the hills*";

and the resolute consistency which maintains and vindicates her passion and her freedom is throughout at once natural and heroic.

We have not time to enlarge furthur on the scope or the details of the poem, on its merits of character and language, its qualities of thought and emotion. We will only refer, for one instance among others of clear and vigorous description, to the account of the passage of the Alps—

> "*peaks that rose in storm*
> *To hold the stars, or catch the morn, or keep*
> *The evening with a splendour of regret;*
>
> * * * * * *
>
> *On dawn-swept heights the war-cry of the winds,*
> *The wet wrath round the steaming battlements,*
> *From which the sun leapt upward, like a sword*
> *Drawn from its scabbard;"*

and for one example of not less simple or less forcible drawing of character, to the sketch of Archimedes, slain in the mid passion and possession of science; to which the homage here studiously paid by the dramatist who pauses on his rapid way to do it reverence will recall the honoured name of that father to whose memory the poem is inscribed. As an offering worthy of such a name, we receive with all welcome this latest accession to the English school of historic drama.

SIMEON SOLOMON'S 'VISION OF LOVE'

AND OTHER STUDIES

[*The Dark Blue*, July, 1871.]

SIMEON SOLOMON

NOTES ON HIS 'VISION OF LOVE' AND
OTHER STUDIES

IF it may be said with perfect accuracy that in all plastic art, whether the language chosen be of words or forms, of sounds or colours, beauty is the only truth, and nothing not beautiful is true; yet this axiom of a great living artist and critic must not be so construed as to imply forgetfulness of the manifold and multiform nature of beauty. To one interpreter the terror or the pity of it, the shadow or the splendour, will appear as its main aspect, as that which gives him his fittest material for work or speech, the substance most pliable to his spirit, the form most suggestive to his hand; to another its simplicity or its mystery, its community or its specialty of gifts. Each servant serves under the compulsion of his own charm; each spirit has its own chain. Upon men in whom there is, so to speak, a compound genius, an intermixture of spiritual forces, a confluence of separate yet conspiring influences, diverse in source yet congruous in result—upon men in whose eyes the boundary lines of the several conterminous arts appear less as lines of mere distinction than as lines of mutual alliance—the impression of the mystery in all beauty, and in all defects that fall short of it, and in all excesses that overbear it, is likely to have a special hold. The subtle interfusion of art with art, of sound with form, of vocal words with silent colours, is as perceptible to the sense and as inexplicable to the understanding of such men as the interfusion of spirit with flesh is to all men in common; and in fact when perceived of no less significance than this, but rather a part and complement of the same truth. One of such artists, and at once recognizable as such, is Mr. Simeon Solomon. There is not, for instance, more of the painter's art in the verse of Keats than of the musician's in Solomon's designs. As surely as the mystery of beauty—a mystery "most glad and sad," as Chaucer says of a woman's mouth—was done into colour of verse for ever unsurpassable in the odes *To a Nightingale* and on *Melancholy*, so is the same secret wrought into perfect music of outline by the painter. The "unheard melodies," which Keats, with a sense beyond the senses, perceived and enjoyed in the forms of his Grecian urn, vibrate in the forms of this artist's handiwork; and all their lines and colours,

> *Not to the sensual ear, but more endeared,*
> *Pipe to the spirit ditties of no tone.*

Since the first years of his very early and brilliant celebrity as a young artist of high imaginative power and promise, Mr. Solomon has been at work long enough to enable us to define at least certain salient and dominant points of his genius. It holds at once of east and west, of Greek and Hebrew. So much indeed does this fresh interfusion of influences give tone and shape to his imagination, that I have heard him likened on this ground to Heine, as a kindred Hellenist of the Hebrews. Grecian form and beauty divide the allegiance of his spirit with Hebraic shadow and majesty: depths of cloud unsearchable and summits unsurmountable of fire darken and lighten before the vision of a soul enamoured of soft light and clear water, of leaves and flowers and limbs more lovely than these. For no painter has more love of loveliness; but the fair forms of godhead and manhood which in ancient art are purely and merely beautiful rise again under his hand with the likeness on them of a new thing, the shadow of a new sense, the hint of a new meaning; their eyes have seen in sleep or waking, in substance or reflection, some change now past or passing or to come; their lips have tasted a new savour in the wine of life, one strange and alien to the vintage of old; they know of something beyond form and outside of speech. There is a questioning wonder in their faces, a fine joy and a faint sorrow, a trouble as of water stirred, a delight as of thirst appeased. Always, at feast or sacrifice, in chamber or in field, the air and carriage of their beauty has something in it of strange: hardly a figure but has some touch, though never so delicately slight, either of eagerness or of weariness, some note of expectancy or of satiety, some semblance of outlook or inlook: but prospective or introspective, an expression is there which is not pure Greek, a shade or tone of thought or feeling beyond Hellenic contemplation; whether it be oriental or modern in its origin, and derive from national or personal sources. This passionate sentiment of mystery seems at times to "o'erinform its tenement" of line and colour, and impress itself even to perplexity upon the sense of the spectator. The various studies, all full of subtleties and beauties definable and not definable, to which the artist has given for commentary the graceful mysticism of a symbolic rhapsody in prose, are also full to overflowing of such sentiment. Read by itself as a fragment of spiritual allegory, this written *Vision of Love revealed in Sleep* seems to want even that much coherence which is requisite to keep symbolic or allegoric art from absolute dissolution and collapse; that unity of outline and connection of purpose, that gradation of correlative parts and significance of corresponsive details, without which the whole aerial and tremulous fabric of symbolism must decompose into mere confusion of formless and fruitless chaos. Even allegory or prophecy must live and work by rule as well as by rapture; transparent it need not be, but it must be translucent. And translucent the fluctuating twilight of this rhapsody does become in time, with the light behind it of the designs; though at first it seems as hard to distinguish one incarnation of love or sleep or charity from the next following as to disentangle the wings and wheels of Ezekiel's cherubim, or to discover and determine the respective properties and qualities of Blake's "emanations" and "spectres." The style is soft, fluent, genuinely melodious; it has nothing of inflation or constraint. There is almost a superflux of images full of tender colour and subtle grace, which is sure to lead the writer into some danger of confusion and repetition; and in such vague and uncertain ground any such stumbling-blocks are likely to be especial rocks of offence to the feet of the traveller. Throughout the whole there is as it were a suffusion of music, a transpiration of light and sound, very delicately and surely sustained. There are thoughts and fragments of thoughts, fancies and fantastic symbols, sometimes of rare beauty and singular force; in this, for instance, of Night as a mother watching Sleep her child, there is a greater height and sweetness of imagination than in any but the sweetest and highest poetic allegories. "And she, to whom all was as an open scroll, wept when she looked upon him whose heart was as the heart of a little child." The depth and tenderness of this conception of Night, omniscient with the conscience of all things wrought under her shadow, world-wide of sight and sway, and wise with all the world's wisdom, weeping for love over the innocence of her first-born, is great and perfect enough for the noblest verse of a poet. The same affluence and delicacy of emblems interwoven with every part of the allegory is kept up from the first dawn of memory to the last transfiguration of love. There is an exquisite touch in the first vision of Memory standing by the sea-side with the shell held to her ear whose voice "unburied the dead cycles of the soul," with autumn leaves showered on head and breast, "and upon her raiment small flecks of foam had already dried"; this last emblem of the salt small foam-flecks, sharp and arid waifs of the unquiet sea of life, light and bitter strays of barren thought and remembrance with the freshness dried out of them, is beautiful and new. Dim and vague as the atmosphere of such work should be, this vision would be more significant, and not less suggestive of things hidden in secret places of spiritual reserve, if it had more body of drawing, more shapeliness of thought and fixity of outline. Not that we would seek for solidity in shadow, or blame the beauty of luminous clouds for confusion of molten outlines; but even in cloud there is some law of form, some continuous harmony of line and mass, that only dissolves and changes "as a tune into a tune." To invigorate and support this fair frame of allegory there should be some clearer infusion of a purpose; there should be some thread of clearer connection, some filament, though never so slender, to link vision again to vision, some clue, "as subtle as Arachne's broken woof," to lead the reader's perception through the labyrinth of sounds and shapes. Each new revelation and change of aspect has beauty and meaning of its own; but even in a dream the steps of progress seem clearer than here, and the process from stage to stage of action or passion is ruled after some lawless law and irrational reason of its own. Such process as this at least we might hope to find even in the records of allegoric vision; in this mystery or tragedy of the passion of a divine sufferer "wounded in the house of his friends" and bleeding from the hands of men, those who follow the track of his pilgrimage might desire at least to be shown the stations of his cross.

We miss the thread of union between the varying visions of love forsaken and shamed, wounded and forgotten; of guileless and soulless pleasure in its naked and melodious maidenhood, and passion that makes havoc of love, and after that even of itself also; of death and silence, and of sleep and time. Many of these have in them the sweetness and depth of good dreams, and much subtle and various beauty; and had we but some clue to the gradations of its course, we might thread our way through the Dædalian maze with a free sense of gratitude to the artificer whose cunning reared it to hide no monstrous thing, but one of divine likeness. It might have been well to issue with the text some further reproductions of the designs: those especially of the wounded Love from whose heart's blood the roses break into blossom, of Desire with body and raiment dishevelled and deformed from self-inflicted strokes, of Divine Charity bearing Sleep down to the dark earth among men that suffer, of Love upborne by the strong arms and wings of Time, of the spirit that watches in the depth of its crystal sphere the mutable reflections of the world and the revolutions of its hidden things; all designs full of mystical attraction and passion, of bitter sweetness and burning beauty.

Outside the immediate cycle of this legend of love divine and human, the artist has done much other work of a cognate kind; his sketches and studies in this line have always the charm of a visible enjoyment in the vigorous indulgence of a natural taste and power. One of these, a noble study of *Sleepers and One that Watches* has been translated into verse of kindred strength and delicacy, in three fine sonnets of high rank among the clear-cut and exquisite *Intaglios* of Mr. John Payne. But the artist is not a mere cloud-compeller, a dreamer on the wing who cannot use his feet for good travelling purpose on hard ground; witness the admirable picture of Roman ladies at a show of gladiators, exhibited in 1865, which remains still his masterpiece of large dramatic realism and live imagination. All the heads are full of personal force and character, especially the woman's with heavy brilliant hair and glittering white skin, like hard smooth snow against the sunlight, the delicious thirst and subtle ravin of sensual hunger for blood visibly enkindled in every line of the sweet fierce features. Mr. Solomon apparently has sufficient sense of physiology to share the theory which M. Alphonse Karr long since proposed to develop at length in a systematic treatise "sur la férocité des blondes." The whole spirit of this noble picture is imbued with the proper tragic beauty and truth and terror.

As the Hebrew love of dim vast atmosphere and infinite spiritual range without foothold on earth or resting-place in nature is perceptible in the mystic and symbolic cast of so many sketches and studies, so is a certain loving interest in the old sacred forms, in the very body of historic tradition, made manifest in various more literal designs of actual religious offices. One series of such represents on a small scale, with singular force and refinement, the several ceremonies of the sacred seasons and festivals of the Jewish year. Other instances of this ceremonial bias towards religious forms of splendour or solemnity are frequent in the list of the painter's works; gorgeous studies of eastern priests in church or synagogue, of young saint and rabbi and Greek bishop doing their divine service in "full-blown dignity" of official magic. I remember faces among them admirable for holy heaviness of feature and sombre stolidity of sanctitude. No Venetian ever took truer delight in glorious vestures, in majestic embroideries, in the sharp deep sheen and glowing refraction of golden vessels; none of them ever lusted more hotly after the solid splendours of metal and marble, the grave glories of purple raiment and gleaming cup or censer. This same magnificence gives tone and colour to his classic subjects which explains their kinship to designs apparently so diverse in aim. Modern rather than classical, as we have noticed, in sentiment and significance, they combine the fervent violence of feeling or faith which is peculiar to the Hebrews with the sensitive acuteness of desire, the sublime reserve and balance of passion, which is peculiar to the Greeks. Something of Ezekiel is here mixed with something of Anacreon; here the Anthology and the Apocalypse have each set a distinct mark: the author of the Canticles and the author of the Atys have agreed for a while to work together. The grievous and glorious result of aspiration and enjoyment is here legible; the sadness that is latent in gladness; the pleasure that is palpable in pain. Fixed eyes and fervent lips are full of divine disquiet and instinctive resignation. All the sorrow of the senses is incarnate in the mournful and melodious beauty of those faces; they have learnt to abstain from wishing; they are learning to abstain from hope. Especially in such works as the *Sappho* and the *Antinous* of some years since does this unconscious underlying sense assert itself. The wasted and weary beauty of the one, the faultless and fruitful beauty of the other, bear alike the stamp of sorrow; of perplexities unsolved and desires unsatisfied. They are not the divine faces familiar to us: the lean and dusky features of this Sappho are unlike those of her traditional bust, so clear, firm, and pure; this Antinous is rather like Ampelus than Bacchus. But the heart and soul of these pictures none can fail to recognise as right; and the decoration is in all its details noble and significant. The clinging arms and labouring lips of Sappho, her fiery pallor and swooning eyes, the bitter and sterile savour of subsiding passion which seems to sharpen the mouth and draw down the eyelids, translate as far as colour can translate her. The face and figure beside her are soulless and passive, the beauty inert as a flower's; the violent spirit that aspires, the satisfied body that takes rest, are here seen as it were in types; the division of pure soul and of mere flesh; the powerful thing that lives without peace, and the peaceful thing that vegetates without power. In *The Sacrifice of Antinous*, he officiates before the god under the divine disguise of Bacchus himself; the curled and ample hair, the pure splendour of faultless cheek and neck, the leopard-skin and thyrsus, are all of the god, and godlike; the mournful wonderful lips and eyes are coloured with mortal blood and lighted with human vision. In these pictures some obscure suppressed tragedy of thought and passion and fate seems latent as the vital veins under a clear skin. Intentionally or not as it may be, some utter sorrow of soul, some world-old hopelessness of heart, mixed with the strong sweet sense of power and beauty, has here been cast afresh into types. Elsewhere again, as in an earlier drawing which my remembrance makes much of, this dim tragic undertone is absent. The two ministering maidens in the Temple of Venus are priestesses of no sad god, preachers of no sad thing. They have not seen beyond the day's beauty, nor desired a delight beyond the hour's capacity to give. As the Epithalamium of Catullus to his Atys, so is this bright and sweet drawing to the Sappho. Here all is clear red and pale white, the serene and joyful colours of pure marble and shed rose-leaves: there dim green and shadows of dusky gray surround and sadden the splendour of fair faces and bright limbs. This artist affects soft backgrounds of pale southern foliage and the sudden slim shoots of a light southern spring; these often give the keynote to his designs, always adding to them a general grace of shape and gravity of tone as unmistakable as any other special quality of work. But here nothing is deeper or darker than the fallen petals which spot the fair pavement of the temple. One girl, white-robed and radiant as white water-flowers, has half let fall the rose that droops in her hand, dropping leaf by leaf like tears; both have the languor and the fruitful air of flowers in a sultry place; their leaning limbs and fervent faces are full of the goddess; their lips and eyes allure and await the invisible attendant Loves. The clear pearl-white cheeks and tender mouths have still about them the subtle purity of sleep; the whole drawing has upon it the heavy incumbent light of summer but half awake. Nothing of more simple and brilliant beauty has been done of late years. Here the spirit of joy is pure and whole; but a spirit more common is that which foresees without eyes and forehears without ears the far-off features and the soundless feet of change; such a spirit as dictated the choice of subject in a picture of two young lovers in fresh fulness of first love crossed and troubled visibly by the mere shadow and the mere breath of doubt, the dream of inevitable change to come which dims the longing eyes of the girl with a ghostly foreknowledge that this too shall pass away, as with arms half clinging and half repellent she seems at once to hold off and to hold fast the lover whose bright youth for the moment is smiling back in the face of hers—a face full of the soft fear and secret certitude of future things which I have tried elsewhere to render in the verses called *Erotion* written as a comment on this picture, with design to express the subtle passionate sense of mortality in love itself which wells up from "the middle spring of pleasures," yet cannot quite kill the day's delight or eat away with the bitter poison of doubt the burning faith and self-abandoned fondness of the hour; since at least, though the future be for others, and the love now here turn elsewhere to seek pasture in fresh fields from other flowers, the vows and kisses of these his present lips are not theirs but hers, as the memory of his love and the shadow of his youth shall be hers for ever.

In such designs the sorrow is simple as the beauty, the spirit simple as the form; in others there is all the luxury and mystery of southern passion and eastern dream. Many of these, as the figure bearing the eucharist of love, have a supersexual beauty, in which the lineaments of woman and of man seem blended as the lines of sky and landscape melt in burning mist of heat and light. Others, as the Bacchus, have about them a fleshly glory of godhead and bodily deity, which holds at once of earth and heaven; neither the mystic and conquering Indian is this god, nor the fierce choregus of Cithæron. The artist's passionate love of gorgeous mysteries, "prodigious mixtures and confusions strange" of sense and spirit no less than " of good and ill," has given him the will and the power to spiritualise at his pleasure, by the height and splendour of his treatment, the somewhat unspiritual memory of Heliogabalus, *Emperor of Rome and High Priest of the Sun*, symbolic in that strange union of offices at once of east and west, of ghostly glory and visible lordship, of the lusts of the flesh and the secrets of the soul, of the kingdom of this world and the mystery of another: the superb and luxurious power and subtlety of the study take in both aspects of his figure, the strangest surely that ever for an instant overtopped the world.

There is an entire class of Mr. Solomon's designs in which the living principle and moving spirit is music made visible. His groups of girls and youths that listen to one singing or reciting seem utterly imbued with the spirit of sound, clothed with music as with a garment, kindled and swayed by it as fire or as foliage by a wakening wind. In pictures where no one figures as making music, the same fine inevitable sense of song makes melodies of vocal colour and symphonies of painted cadence. The beautiful oil painting of bride, bridegroom, and paranymph has in its deep ripe tones the same suffusion of sound as that of the evening hymn to the hours; the colours have speech in them, a noble and solemn speech, and full of large strong harmonies. In the visible "mystery of faith" we feel the same mighty measures of a silent song go up with the elevation of the host; and from the soundless lips of Love and Sleep, of Memory and of Dreams, of Pleasure and Lust and Death, the voice of their manifold mystery is audible.

In almost all of these there is perceptible the same profound suggestion of unity between opposites, the same recognition of the identity of contraries. Even in the gatherings of children about the knees of Love, as he tells his first tales to elder and younger lads and girls, there are touches of trouble and distraction, of faint doubt and formless pain on the fresh earnest faces that attend in wonder and in trance. Even in the glad soft grouping of boys and maidens by " summer twilight," under light bloom of branches that play against a gracious gleaming sky, their clear smiles and swift chance gestures recall some thought of the shadow as well as the light of life; and always there seems to rise up before the spirit, at thought of the might and ravage of time and "sad mortality," the eternal question—

> *How with this rage shall beauty hold a plea,*
> *Whose action is no stronger than a flower?*

But far other questions than this rise up behind it, as we gaze into the great and terrible mystery of beauty, and turn over in thought the gloss of far other commentators, the scrolls of strange interpreters, materialist and mystic. In the features of these groups and figures which move and make music before us in the dumb show of lines and colours, we see the latent relations of pain and pleasure, the subtle conspiracies of good with evil, the deep alliances of death and life, of love and hate, of attraction and abhorrence. Whether suffering or enjoyment be the master expression of a face, and whether that enjoyment or that suffering be merely or

mainly spiritual or sensual, it is often hard to say—
hard often to make sure whether the look of loveliest
features be the look of a cruel or a pitiful soul.
Sometimes the sensible vibration as of living lips and
eyes lets out the secret spirit, and we see the springs
of its inner and confluent emotions. The subtleties
and harmonies of suggestion in such studies of
complex or it may be perverse nature would have
drawn forth praise and sympathy from Baudelaire,
most loving of all students of strange beauty and
abnormal refinement, of painful pleasures of soul and
inverted raptures of sense. There is a mixture of
utmost delicacy with a fine cruelty in some of these
faces of fair feminine youth which recalls the explana-
tion of a philosopher of the material school, whose
doctrine is at least not without historic example and
evidence to support it : " Une infinité de sots, dupes
de cette incroyable sensibilité qu'ils voient dans les
femmes, ne se doutent pas que les extrémités se rapproch-
ent, et que c'est précisément au foyer de ce sentiment
que la cruauté prend sa source. Parce que *la cruauté
n'est elle-même qu'une des branches de la sensibilité*, et
que c'est toujours en raison du degré dont nos âmes
en sont pénétrées que les grandes horreurs se
commettent." The matter of this passage is better
than the style ; by the presence of this element we
may distinguish cruelty from brutality, a Nero from a

Gallifet, a Brinvilliers from a "baby-farmer." In several of Mr. Solomon's designs we find heads emblematic of active or visionary passion upon which the seal of this sensitive cruelty is set; made beautiful beyond the beauty of serpent or of tiger by the sensible infusion of a soul which refines to a more delicate delight the mere nervous lust after blood, the mere physical appetite and ravenous relish for fleshly torture; which finds out the very "spirit of sense" and fine root of utmost feeling alike in the patient and the agent of the pain. There are no bestial faces, no mere vile types of brutality, but only of this cunning and cruel sensibility which catches fire from the stroke it deals, and drinks as its wine of life the blood of its sentient sacrifice. The poignancy of this pleasure is patent and fervent in the face of the fair woman overlooking the fresh full agony in the circus; the aftertaste of fierce weariness and bitter languor that corrodes the soul is perceptible in the aspect of the figure representing Lust, with haunted eyes and savage haggard lips and barren body scored with blood, in the allegoric design of Love. Other faces again are live emblems of an infinite tenderness, of sad illimitable pity, of the sweetness of utter faith and ardour that consumes all the meaner elements of life; the fiery passion and hunger after God of St. Theresa, who might be taken as patroness of the Christian side of this painter's art: one whole class of his religious designs is impregnated with the burning mysticism and raging rapture of her visions, reflected as we feel them in Crashaw's hymn of invocation from the furnace of her own fierce words and phrases of prostrate ardour and amorous appeal to her Bridegroom.

All great and exquisite colourists have a mystery of their own, the conscience of a power known to themselves only as the heart knows its own bitterness, and not more communicable or explicable. In this case the pictorial power is so mixed with personal quality, so informed and suffused with a subtle energy of sentiment, that a student from without may perhaps be able to note, not quite inaccurately or unprofitably, the main spiritual elements of the painter's work. In the work of some artists the sentiment is either a blank or a mist; and none but technical criticism of such work can be other than incompetent and injurious. The art of Mr. Solomon is of a kind which has inevitable attraction for artists of another sort, and is all the more liable to suffer from the verdicts of unskilled and untrained judgments. But an artist of his rank and quality has no need to cry out against the rash intrusion of critical stragglers from the demesne of any other art. He can afford the risk of such sympathies, for his own is rich in the qualities of those others also, in musical and poetic excellence not less positive than the pictorial; and as artist he stands high enough to be above all chance of the imputation cast on some that they seek comfort in the ignorant admiration and reciprocal sympathy of men who cultivate some alien line of art, for conscious incompetence and failure in their own; fain to find shelter for bad painting under the plea of poetic feeling, or excuse for bad verse under the plea of good thought or sentiment. By right of his innate energies and actual performances, he claims kinship and alliance with the foremost in all fields of art, while holding in his own a special and memorable place. Withdrawn from the roll of artists, his name would leave a void impossible to fill up by any worthiest or ablest substitute; by any name of master in the past or disciple in the present or future. The one high test requisite for all genuine and durable honour is beyond all question his; he is himself alone, and one whose place no man can take. They only, but they assuredly, of whom this can be said, may trust in their life to come. Time wears out the names of the best imitators and followers; but he whose place is his own, and that place high among his fellows, may be content to leave his life's work with all confidence to time.

LONDON:

Printed for THOMAS J. WISE, Hampstead, N.W.

Edition limited to Thirty-two Copies.